The Little Boy Who Wouldn't Eat Cheesecake

Written by **Christina Myers**   Illustrated by **Katherine Carver**

Humble & Bold Press - Atlanta
www.humbleandbold.com

To my father-in-law, Roger,
thanks for the wonderful dinners and for sharing this
sweet story from your childhood.

To my husband, Scott,
thank you for your endless encouragement throughout this adventure.
What a wild ride!

And to my younger son, Asa Daniel,
and other children who will soon read about
The Little Boy Who Wouldn't Eat Cheesecake
ENJOY!

The Little Boy Who Wouldn't Eat Cheesecake Text copyright © 2020 by Christina Myers Illustrations copyright © 2020 by Katherine Carver All rights reserved. No part of this publication may be reproduced, distributed, or transmitted in any form, in whole or in part, by any means, including, but not limited to, electronic, graphic or mechanical, photocopying, recording, or by any information storage retrieval system without the prior written permission of the copyright owners, except in the case of brief quotations embodied in critical reviews and certain other noncommercial uses permitted by copyright law. For permission requests, write to Christina@humbleandbold.com, the copyright owner.

Special thanks to Hardin Communications.

Publisher's Cataloging-In-Publication Data
(Prepared by The Donohue Group, Inc.)

Names: Myers, Christina (Christina W.), author. | Carver, Katherine, illustrator.
Title: The little boy who wouldn't eat cheesecake / written by Christina Myers, illustrated by Katherine Carver.
Description: Atlanta : Humble & Bold Press, [2020] | Interest age level: 004-009. | Summary: "While World War II is changing the world in major ways, a young boy named Roger finds himself in a different kind of fight--a battle within himself--as he tries to muster up the courage to sample a bite of cheesecake. Yes, that's right, cheesecake. You see, Roger can't understand how cheese, regularly eaten in his grilled sandwiches, could possibly taste good in cake. He is quite disturbed that others not only find this oddity acceptable but also say it's delicious. The Little Boy Who Wouldn't Eat Cheesecake inspires picky eaters and young readers, ages 4-9, to try new things and encourages conversation with older family members and friends about foods they didn't like in childhood (or, at least, thought they didn't like) and what happened when they actually tried the foods for themselves!"-- Provided by publisher.
Identifiers: ISBN 9781735019222 (hardcover) | ISBN 9781735019215 (softcover) | ISBN 9781735019208 (EPUB) | ISBN 9781735019239 (MOBI)
Subjects: LCSH: Food preferences in children--Juvenile fiction. | Food habits--Psychological aspects--Juvenile fiction. | World War, 1939-1945--Psychological aspects--Juvenile fiction. | Cooking (Cheese)--Juvenile fiction. | CYAC: Food preferences in children--Fiction. | Food habits--Psychological aspects--Fiction. | World War, 1939-1945--Psychological aspects--Fiction. | Cooking (Cheese)--Fiction.
Classification: LCC PZ7.1.M92 Li 2020 (print) | LCC PZ7.1.M92 (ebook) | DDC [E]--dc23

Library of Congress Control Number: 2020909048

Humble & Bold Press - Atlanta
www.humbleandbold.com

On special occasions, Roger Myers likes to take his wife, children, and grandchildren out to a nice restaurant, and he always wears his stylish fedora. His family calls him Papa.

After dinner, Papa grins and asks his grandkids, "Hey! Have you guys ever heard the story about the little boy who wouldn't eat cheesecake?" Joshua, Hannah, and Rex smile at each other and giggle because they've heard the story many times. Still, they listen.

"Well, here it goes! Back in the early forties, when I was about your age and living in Chattanooga, Tennessee, my parents and I would go downtown to Gula's restaurant every Sunday after church."

After the meal, my parents would always ask me if I would like to have some New York cheesecake for dessert. Every time, I would scrunch my nose and politely reply, "No, thank you."

My father would ask if I was sure, and without much thought, I'd always reply, "Yes!"

"Well, I just know that I won't," I said, with my arms folded. *When I cross my arms like this, it means that I am serious.*

"But why?" my father asked, "Can you please explain to me how you are so sure that you do not like cheesecake?"

"Well, I like cheese in sandwiches, but cheese in cake just doesn't sound good to me."

My father explained, "Son, the cheese in the cheesecake is not like the cheese that is in your grilled cheese sandwiches."

"The cheese in cheesecake is vanilla white and creamy. In the cake it tastes sweet."

"What?" I exclaimed, "How can cheese be sweet?" I always thought cheese was an orangish color and salty.

"Son, the cheese isn't sweet by itself. You add sugar! Sugar is what makes the cake sweet."

"Oh! Well, I'll think about it, but I don't want any today."

My parents looked at each other and smiled, like parents do when they know something that you don't. *You need to be on alert when you see your parents smile at each other in that funny way.*

The next Sunday, I watched my parents more closely as they ate their cheesecake. I couldn't help but notice how they smiled after each bite. I waited for my father to ask me if I wanted to try a piece, but he didn't this time.

"Dad, you forgot to ask me if I wanted to try a bite of cheesecake!" I reminded him.

My father smiled and said, "I didn't forget. I know that when you're ready, you will try it . . . perhaps when you are older?"

On the way home, I started to feel like I should have at least tried a small bite of the cheesecake. But how can cheese taste sweet? This was awful! What should I do?

The next day, I made a very important decision, the type of decision someone makes once they are older. After all, I was now older than I was the day before, and I even felt older. I waited all day for my father to come home from work so I could tell him the big news.

Finally, my father arrived. Before he could get out of the car, I was standing right outside, ready with the big announcement: "This Sunday, I will try a bite of the cheesecake!"

My father gave me a big smile. He leaned down to my level and said, "Son, I'm so glad that you have decided to try something new."

"Not a whole piece, just a little bite," I said.

My father chuckled, "Okay. Well, I guess a little bite is better than no bite at all."

Feeling happy with myself, I looked forward to the big day. I was growing older, making big decisions, and would soon find out if I really didn't like cheesecake, once and for all.

Well, before I knew it, Sunday was upon us, and we were back at Gula's for lunch.

I could hardly enjoy my meal because my thoughts began to worry.

What if the cheesecake is yucky and awful? What if it makes me sick and I pass out? Boy! This is a bad idea!

The big moment arrived. The waiter brought over my parents' cheesecake and gently placed it on the table.

I will just put on a brave face, swallow very quickly, and wash it down with my milk or water, whichever is closer, I thought.

While staring at the cheesecake, I picked up my dessert fork ever so slowly. I lightly dipped my fork into the cheesecake, taking only a small piece.

While bringing it to my mouth, I decided to hold my nose and close one eye. My fork edged closer and closer to my mouth and then suddenly froze.

I saw the fork bravely disappear into my mouth. My parents waited with anticipation, as my taste buds voted. *Wow! Mmm!* I thought. "Hey, this is good!" I proclaimed.

My parents laughed with excitement and said in unison, "Yes, we've been trying to tell you!"

For the rest of the long week, I looked forward to having the cheesecake again.

I was feeling older, making such big decisions.

Finally, Sunday had come, and we were back at Gula's. I was excited, ready to order my cheesecake.

When the waiter came over, he had very bad news: "I'm sorry, folks, but we are all out of cheesecake, and will be for some time. Due to the war, sugar has been rationed. However, we still have a couple of slices of carrot cake available. Would anyone care for some delicious carrot cake?"

My father looked at me with a smile, as I made a perplexed face. *How can a carrot in cake be good? Should I try it?* I thought.

"And that's the story of the little boy who wouldn't eat cheesecake!" Papa said with a grin. "Now... hopefully, you guys won't make the same mistake I did, by waiting too late to try something new.

"So, who wants cheesecake for dessert?"

Oh, taste and see that the
LORD is good!
Psalm 34:8 (ESV)

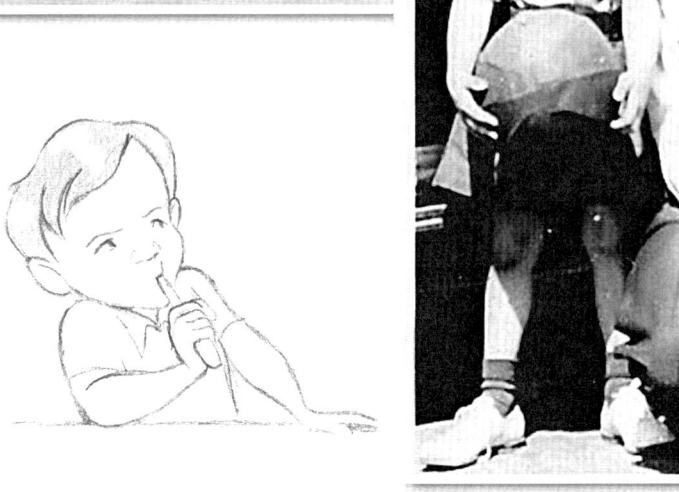

For more on this story visit
www.humbleandbold.com

Christina Myers is a Southern blogger, screenwriter, and speaker, with a background in voice-over work and acting. She enjoys sharing the Good News and encouraging others while pursuing many creative interests at humbleandbold.com. She has taught children for many years and lives in the suburbs of Atlanta with her husband, Scott, and their two sons, Rex and Asa. This is her first children's book to be published.

As a child, Christina also wondered how cheese in cake could ever be sweet, so when she heard her father-in-law, Roger, tell this story, she knew she had to share it with others. Adding a comical twist at the end.

Katherine Carver is a dreamer, cartoonist, animator, and writer. Her motto: keep going and never give up. She assisted Christina in teaching art to children at Perimeter Church in Johns Creek, Georgia. Now residing in the suburbs of Chattanooga, Tennessee, she uses her creativity to bring characters to life using her gift of illustrative art. Katherine is a big believer in taking risks.

Made in United States
North Haven, CT
21 January 2023

31439498R00020